For a Poet's Wunderkammer

For a Poet's Wunderkammer

Lynn Fullington

authorHOUSE®

AuthorHouse™
1663 Liberty Drive
Bloomington, IN 47403
www.authorhouse.com
Phone: 1-800-839-8640

Published by AuthorHouse   08/15/2012

ISBN: 978-1-4772-6007-4 (sc)
ISBN: 978-1-4772-6078-4 (e)

Library of Congress Control Number: 2012914749

Any people depicted in stock imagery provided by Thinkstock are models, and such images are being used for illustrative purposes only.
Certain stock imagery © Thinkstock.

This book is printed on acid-free paper.

Because of the dynamic nature of the Internet, any web addresses or links contained in this book may have changed since publication and may no longer be valid. The views expressed in this work are solely those of the author and do not necessarily reflect the views of the publisher, and the publisher hereby disclaims any responsibility for them.

Acknowledgements

. . . of knowing looks, hearty laughs and thoughtful comments From Margaret, Carol, Jon, Julie, George, and John.
A most appreciated collaboration.

Watching Words Go By
         Published by Pogonip Feb. 1997

A Current, A Thistle, A Scuffed Stone, A Corkscrew, A Pair of Matched-Sighs, A Cricket, Peacocks, A Stetson, A Chased Rose, Wunderkammer Warehouse, Published by Snakeskin 1997 to 2012.

An Eighteen Wheeler
         Published by BuzzWords Feb. 2000

For a Poet's
WUNDERKAMMER

A Question

Tell me, which would you rather see
A shatzkammer of treasure,
A kuntzhammer of objects d'art
or a collection for a wunderkammer?
All three possibilities so small
they stand as cabinets on four graceful legs.
The nobleman's doll house with all
the items he would have carried
in his pockets, were he a child.

A poet's curio cabinet would be objects
conferring poetry through a person's eyes.
Things that make words
stand up and take notice. And placed
thereafter in this small setting to evoke
the pleasures of one's life. . .

A curio cabinet of the objects of our love.
Miniature deserts,
Small chili restaurants,
and inch high roller coasters that
tested our nerve and our poetic lives.
Miniature poetry books in leather bindings
piled in every corner and you closer than
my very own heart

Collecting

The Plight of the Collector

It's beautiful! Some craftwise soul
loved wood, loved carving, loved birds
and you who have never seen such a bird
can collect it
That act alone confers Creator on you.

A daring act placing it on a shelf
all by itself. A one-of-a-kind decoy
with dust and time
robbing it of it's familiars,
its surroundings, the live ones
that fly in and settle around it.
Yet your specious satisfaction

in one-for-safe-keeping goes on.
You re-route your way, looking
everyday after daily affairs

for duck ponds, inside
woodcarvers shops, or
scanning skies over botanical gardens
but those chosen to be collected,
know the fate on an empty shelf
keep to themselves, hoping they're
"not special enough."

A bird sanctuary beckons
where birds voluntarily collect
--a comforting match
for some one collecting. Still
the last crane
touching down objected.

"It's all or nothing" was the declaration.
"A fine flock, taken all together.
May not be all equal to the one on the shelf.
Give up selecting, accept us,
a collection of feathers
on a temporary stop."

You smile, the solution is so obvious.
Elite-ism finally overturned!
You will collect flocks.

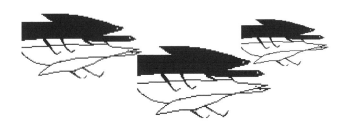

Then, all are welcome if they fly
in formation--stretching their necks,
trailing their feet.
They are to occupy the shelf
with the unique bird of its kind.
Temporary is the only stumbling block.

They take off and land with the freedom
of endangered species, not enough conviction
by even one bird to talk wooden
and learn the knack
of surviving uniquely.

The Plight of One Collected

The shelf remained empty except
for the hand-crafted Duxbury Peep
from northern coastal shores.
He stood tirelessly
on a stick, confident he could lure
others more alive,
but stay prim and trim
despite the giant shapes
that bent over him on the shelf.

All beings savor a sense of purpose.
No grain, without dedication
for strengthening the wood,
obstructing the knife
from a cross-wise direction.

No pride left--- if left unpolished,
unable to blend surface
to internal tensions. And when
these desires are fulfilled the world
of menacing shapes stand in awe
of a perfect wood piece.

But this one stood painted.
What hope now? Purpose replaced. Painted,
standing on a shelf. A historical displacement
from attracting birds, no longer on shore
to lure visitors, alone on a shelf
with cranes coming and going and
Feathers that could not be preened.

The Uncertainty of the Viewer

If their curiosity is alive and well
they might wonder at the "party
of birds" ---a reasonable term
if you didn't know what to call
a "departure of cranes."

These, the viewer might suspect,
thought nothing
of returning to such a small space,
of the shrinking required for landing.
This was accepted matter-of-factly

but he couldn't help asking:
Why a decoy in your wunderkammer?
Already birds come in endless dozens?

Because his name is unhesitatingly Peep,
became the answer for Questioner of Sunsets.

Because he is man-made.
Because, tomorrow
he will stand unique, alone on the shelf
inciting poems
ad I am a collector of poems.

A Scuffed Stone

I scuffed a stone
that had not fared well in my driveway.
Being too large for my graded
stone lawn, the first to be thrown
by the children waiting for the bus.

And yes,   now --was scuffed.
Its complaint was low,
a non-hysterical misery
that deserved my attention.

Maybe once a granite boulder
in the Pyrenees,
watching millions of slow centuries,
with no particular concern, when
one small storm upset that hill, set tree
and stones rolling toward the town.
The boulder became an obstruction
on the road, then a shield for gunfire
piece by piece, till one crept between
a condor's toes, and traveled vast spaces.

It was better than waiting for erosion--
ending up on an ocean floor.

Yet this was serious. These monumental
beginnings, endurance while time was lost.
Significance worn down to a mere scuffing.
I picked up the stone. All possible, I thought
looking at the smooth surface,
too small for the finish
reserved for monuments,
yet the toe-gripped form of stubborn granite
spoke with patterns of crystalized eloquence.

I put it in my pocket for days
when things did not go right.

*. . . But to me, who knows what it
really is, its transformation makes no matter,
for I will have it repaired in the first village
where I can find a smith, in such a way that
it will not be surpassed or even equaled by the
one that gods of smiths himself made and
forged for the god of battles.*

Don Quixote

A Corkscrew

On the upper most shelf lay
an ancient rust-inlaid corkscrew
known to facilitate the Great Flight
into each New Year.
A fearsome weapon in Quixotic hands
to pin whoresome giants
against the wall.

Its broad handle of precious woods
from great-limbed trees found around
enchanted lakes.
It's twisted hook, the ultimate
in Toledo blades
providing the driving force of revenge
against resolutions that didn't work out.

For some, their tasks had seemed a call
to carry cats to water--
their tails knotted, a fight
to the drowning of cherished ambitions.

For others   New Year's resolutions
sparked a ribald humor at the futile
attempts around them.
And always the glum reminder
that the twist might come undone

and pieces of cork float
in almost every glass.
But the corkscrew was a wonder
in the hands of those who saw
radiant planets in universes ahead
and sparkling tokens
of a true love's favor

And next year's
whoresome giants pinned
against the wall

Are those the faces of love,
those pale irretrievables?
Is it for such I agitate my heart?

Sylvia Plath

A Matched-Pair of Sighs

I found a matched-pair of sighs
overhead, caught in a web--
first over heard and then sighted.
Rainbow hues so resilient
you could barely see through them
to the spider at its weaving.

Sighs, time-bound and
unable to escape the strands
so elegantly fastened to the door.
Silk and silver in the moonlight,
golden wire in autumn.
The sighs came from departures,
an unhurried and mournful taste
on the tongue.

How to detach these fragile sounds
And convey them to a poet's
Wunderkammer where lightly tethered
Sighs and web could wait together
---for those who never return.

A caution to those who gaze
And allow sighs to go uncollected.

The little mute boy was
looking for his voice.
The king of crickets had it . . .

Federico Garcia Lorca

A Cricket

I have a cricket in my collection
Mine has always been a poet
with his stridulations.
Though he remains silent
on most things.

His metal legs, small
yet like huge cranes
on the loading docks
gives out a tinny sound,
only two inches high
that would be deeper
if the legs could move freely.
But sound it has,
That resonates easily when tapped.
I admire that in poets.

The antennae in wire loops above
his head could never be mistaken
for something that must be taken out
and shot. And I was grateful for that.
There is too much pain for voices
unaccustomed to our world.

And the wings or was it the tail end
that Arts Nouveau artists used without
flinching for parallel lines?
So modern, so streamlined
it gave away the cricket's age.

That does not concern this
poet who sees the world from
a command position above
my video screen. When he
cares to comment---*I do not know
where my poems come from.*
Then I ask to write the poems down.

For everything speaks in the universe.
There is nothing that does not
have its language.

La Fontaine

Watching Words Go By

was not hypothetical.
The evidence
was everywhere, soft lines
around the eyes
that heard and sent
the words back.

If only for a few short moments
the passageway was undisturbed.
But when the next words came
eyes widened, and breathing
was withheld.
What was once artful,
was now coldly unpleasant.

You've seen such words
hang in mid-air,
the ground snatched from
under them.
Looking desperately for
other meanings

too far from home to risk returning.
Therefore must flowers stem their talk.
So vulnerable to
perfumed air they could
hardly bare to see words
praising their blossoms
sneered at. Seeing is
exchanged for hearing
in the talk
between the taciturn gardener,
the watering can
and the cyclamen.

Even a rusty nail I once knew
quit scarring
a fine floor, the only
words possible
in the face of total
disregard.

And then it deliberately rolled
into harm's way.
Now, what's left is the talk
Of ever-lasting gouges
and a case of blood
poisoning for those
who will only talk to flowers

Words Returned

The woman stared at her poem
and waited for the ants to come.
She waited for them to bring
the words they had carried away
the night before
when she was too sleepy
to use them.

Soon ants began returning the words
but they were broken
from all that travel
down the wall, through the plaster
and out into desert-dry land.
They dropped them
where they found them.
These had been too abstract
to carry underground
even if they were in pieces.

Above ground,
they were indigestible
except in poems

A Current

Feathers on their way down
give air currents their legitimacy.

You might have felt currents on days
that were both hot and dry
with the unexpected pleasure
in their repartee.
But a feather lets you see
their movement;
their change of temperament
from capricious capsizing
to total neglect
that leaves feathers adrift.

I could be happy as that feather
viewing the world
from east to west,
from top or bottom,
not counting on a landing

But rather catching that
symbiotic relationship
where happiness is concerned.
No regrets because sorrows did not
make me wiser. I have learned
To ride the current.

A Thistle

A thistle drowned its tears in the wind.
All hope gone for a reed-like sound
to travel with its seedy wisps,
 without sounds even grasses could make.
Then the wind would notice a thistle's aire so fragile
it would have to stop to hear. But no wind could.

A wind's bluster never stops. No wind could
help but flatter and pollinate the charming wind
 flower, drive thin straws thru wood, but for fragile
 thistle down there was to be no sound.
Golden finch eat the seed, let the thistle bird make
sounds. Let thistles ride the wind, weeds yet wisps.

Europe knew winds, and sea-crossing wisps
choking both pasture and horse but no wind could
stop the spiny leaf, the creeping root to make
all but Scots regret the soundless thistle. The wind
like history, hurried on ignoring sounds
of homeless seeds, outcasts and the fragile.

Scottish Knights of The Thistle defend the fragile
perhaps even Our Lady's Thistle wisps.
Bagpipes proved Scots could handle any sound
something only diurnal winds could.
Let thistles have their light freedom on the wind
and their scourge of pasture lands below to make

the wind regret sounds thistles could not make.
The Stuart's Thistle no longer fragile
became the national flower intimidating the wind.
Just as ambitious poetic sounds are wisps
until some poet defends them as no wind could
with the prickly leaves of rhyming sound

choking out all other sounds
keeping wary walkers hesitating to make
the rhyme stop. No wind could
stop to admire thoughts so fragile
in the best of hands. Unsung wisps
of new sounds, bagpipes take a second wind.

The hardy mind spreads a poet's sound,
for all the thoughtful hearts no longer fragile.

 It took wisps, historic and proud, to make
thistles content with soundless wisps

And be the delight of poets as no wind could
find sounds that were no longer wind-bound.

A curio cabinet with objects of love.
Miniature deserts, small chili restaurants,
          and inch-high roller coasters that
tested our nerve and our poetic lives.
Miniature poetry books in leather bindings
          piled in every corner
          and you closer than
          my very own heart . . .
                    from *A Question*

Peacocks

When the peacocks called,
in a voice unlovely to the touch
I called back encouraging them
to tell me, a perfect stranger
how they kept pools of moonlight
polished, with silver mines
no longer in operation.
And how they kept a million voices,
fire-flies in stereo, flying
formations through the dark
and all surfaces
gleaming
unreservedly.

I turned to the enigma beside me
What can you tell me about love?

What can you tell me
of love's slow or sudden discovery?
of it's loss and length of recovery,
speedy or delayed
that leaves an echo
like a taste in your mouth.

What can you tell me
that leaves me shakened
from the hearing?
Except that it has happened to you
and that my eyes
are exceptionally blue.

Volcanoes

We picked up mementoes
from each of our five
naked-eye planets,
rocks that melted
under our feet when
kisses turned us to cinders.
And when we lined them up
on the shelf,
each with their shadows,
each took on a different color
from lacquered reds to iridescent blues.
And we relived the heat
of those moments when stars
were no longer needed.
Love, for volcanoes to envy.

I keep my countenance,
I remain self-possessed
Except when a street piano,
*   mechanical and tired*
Reiterates some worn-out common song . .
.

T.S. Eliot

A Half-way Lizard

What if the sun were to open it's vacant eye
 on this world? Would it see green and blue
 where as the others orbiting are only rocky,
 heat-seared, and frozen?
Would it watch us circle around,
 in and out of focus
within its dangerous glare?

And would this be our global warming?
Churning up storms, drying up deserts,
 misplacing rain?

Would this account for my tempers?
 My dismay?
 Am I on my way to becoming a lizard
 that can stand such solar scrutiny?
 Unable to tell as reptilian,
 one emotion from the other?
 Pray to heaven's sun, that it does not go
 indifferently blind
 and leave me unfinished---neither myself
 nor the lizard pre-destined to be saved.

Chinese Peas

If I serve Chinese peas
for breakfast I don't want to hear
Stir fry? then Where's the sausage?
I want to hear Crisp and green
and How like a pod,
so many the same.

Then you may spit them out
unchewed and aiming
in as many different directions
as you can think of
to overcome the pod and its influence
on your nine to five day.

When you come home
they'll be lined up on your dresser
playing poker,
betting you'll never guess
how they got there.

A Bumble Bee

Even if it takes him a hundred years
to fill his save-for-emergencies pot
 with the window left open
for his transit,
the exuberant bumble bee
is my patron saint

He sits behind his honey pot
with wings and legs outstretched.
Fuzzy and bumbly-round
he contemplates
the empty dipper and never minds--
he's got Cinderella's slipper
hidden in the folds of his baggy pants.
From flower to poetic flower he hunts
for a proper fit, happy as a lark, waiting
for the overflow
of a half-filled honey pot.

Thirty-Two Keys

Thirty-two keys on a clumsy wire ring
Laced through their heads:
shaped like underwater goggles,
like triple punched stove tops,
like unstrung mandolins,
even some square holes in round heads.
All rusted and grimy
and intriguing on their clumsy wire ring.

He found them in a small mountain town
on a back street somewhere
in front of a hotel
that had been torn down.
Keys with shanks long enough
for a two inch door, solid oak --strong
enough to keep paying customers in,
curious intruders out.

Spread on a table
like so many die-cut Chinese characters
inscrutable as to the activities within,
indecipherable to the eye peering
through the lock.

All so innocent with their flat key stems
easily models for ornate
Victorian fences that secured the lawn.
But only one with a blunt end
for hammering into the ground.
Perhaps laying spread-eagle was
their natural stance.

Overlapping and sharp edged,
slyly playing pick up sticks.

But stand them up and they bunch over
miniature passage ways
for very small weddings
of regimental officers
staggering under the pleasures
of pre-nuptial rites.

The history of that rough
mountain town was not clear.
Nor that of the hotel
known as an improper place
for decent town folk.
The keys had no comment.

A Wayward Nut

The squirrel tossed
a nut from the top of a tree,
dropped it down the neck of the boy's father
Who knows his boy's mischievous ways
And decides at that moment
to send the squirrel
To military school in Montana.

The boy sympathizes but
Doesn't say a word as he has
No love for cold weather
And hopes to get acquainted
with some Whales in Florida,
plans he didn't know he had.

We all know the way things
Are supposed to happen
And as long as you don't include
Every detail that's the way
They will be.

A Chair with Four Legs

The truth in concrete things
makes all things knowable.
"The chair has four legs."

Now that you mention it.
Yes, that is true.

"And all four legs will support
both men and women equally."
How well-disposed this chair!
How free of prejudice!

How willing to endure
the complete stranger
when support is needed.
How altruistic is a chair!

And you see the evidence
right here in front of your eyes.

How magnificent
to find the Unified Field
Theory waiting and working;
 Science and Philosophy one.

All things fit our abstractions.
abetted by our language, our whimsical
logic, our childhood stories with
happy endings

so long as confirmed by
concrete reality

And nowhere more appropriately
displayed than in
a poet's Wunderkammer.

A Desert Snail

Who cares if it started out plaster,
an elephant six inches tall. Wonderful
stout legs arched and leaning and a smaller
divit to separate tusks from head.

Upside down the feet, from side to side
were as yet, unseparated. Just a small groove
between the two in front.
But what strange v-shapes kept the legs
together, hobbling the walk no doubt
but a joy in shape and shadow.
Yet this elephant
would never fly, would always be looked
upon with suspicion.

There were to be four more,
even smaller, trailing family-wise
tail by fragile tail
then to be spewed and poured.
But somehow time ran out
and only one was cast.

         The plaster
stayed inside.—the wax was lost
but not the core. And when all was done,
trimmed and lightly buffed with
a leathery hide it was a glorious, patient
creature unable to move. The legs you see
were still beautiful from the bottom.

So it stayed inverted.
Became a desert snail, and like all
mesas in the hot sun, amassing shadows
at its base, heavy shell, heavy tentacula,
it was resigned to
its elephant fate up-side-down.

A Cockatiel Named George

Working in his home office,
Running his feet up and down
The keyboard of his existence on
The short perch between wire-mesh walls.
 He whistles tunes
We are supposed to know
And speaks out frankly
At our inconsequential passing.

The leafy green over his head
Would provide a thoughtful
Cover for his meditation
If ever he should look up.

But while on the job
Up and down, up and down
From perch to perch
He keeps his brightly polished eye
On motes streaming
In on sunshined air.
That is his job.

A Stetson

The disguise reeked of self-doubt.
The overlarge hat with brim that extended
his defensible territory. People ducked to see
eyes cornflower blue, by day or by night.
The hat caused the chin to
point up, easily mistaken
for challenge
and raw courage.

Like the unsmiling surveillance
of plateaus and dust devils,
small specks of travelers
unknown and unwanted.
But quick turns sent hat and wearer
in slightly different directions.
The overlarge shirt hid a shallow chest,
overlarge jeans, despite shrinkage,
 just meant everybody was doing them
---but not hats.

Overlarge Nikes were an exact fit.
Nikes had been the weapons of choice when
teenage justice was sought between classes
and they bloodied the face
of the cattle thief on the floor.
But the hat just rolled its cigarette
                              and moseyed on.

When the hat resided on a chair,
he regarded himself with pride and wonder.
How resolute, how ready for cattle drives
north with days of dusty roads, for survival
beyond the school yard fence.
If only he could live up
to the hat ---never known to acknowledge
deficiencies in any man.

An Eighteen Wheeler

Vanity pulled up in front of the house,
in a huge eighteen wheeler
anticipating the legions of meaningless items
to be moved,
now being sorted inside.
The things they fought over as children
when their ambitions were small.
The bike with the flashy red seat.
Their father with a few spare hairs
and so few hours to spare.
And of course the cookie jar, even
if all the cookies were gone.
All this was meaningless now
but they packed them all up anyway.

The memorabilia of elementary school.
The best seat on the bus,
favorite teachers left behind when
advancing to sixth grade.
And boxes of valentines
from kids they hardly knew
Lost kittens, lost mittens
because they rhymed. Even bullies
bested in the lunch line.
All truly meaningless.
Vanity was running out of space.

High school years with those frantic reports
to prepare for college and life ahead.
Wallet -size pictures
of stringy haired friends, pimply chins
and self-conscious eyes.
Scads of report cards
provoking improvement and yearbooks
proclaiming futures too strange to recount
seeing as to how things turned out.

Things they forgot
until they had to leave their youth
and pack up. Vanity stands on the curb
and determines all was really Vanity.
Nobody breathed a word about "eat, drink
and be merry---

Forget about this "tomorrow"
so you won't have so much to move.

. . its touches of Beauty should never be half way, thereby making the reader breathless instead of content: the rise, the progress, the setting of imagery should like the sun, come natural to him, shine over him, and set soberely although in magnificence, leaving him in the luxury of delight.

John Keats

A Swiss Cuckoo

The ornate little busy body
announces the hour
as it was two centuries ago.
And since the numbers remain
the same one should not be unhappy
if the hours are a bit late.

He stops for the minute
To let us admire his beauty
With the elegant paint stroke
And patterns of colors.
To listen to a voice
That lightens your day
Like the sun that endlessly shines
Leaving us in the luxury of delight

Fresh, Untried Sunday

Here comes Sunday--
A day beyond good and evil
turning one from
the confusion of the week.
The glory of the day held by
the thin thread of now,
an undetermined length since none
have uncoiled this Sunday before.
All the frenzied week hovers elsewhere,
while Sunday swings free,
unbound, unbeholden to anyone.
Just a fresh, untried Sunday.

A Whistle

A whistle by the bed
hanging from the stand of the slender
floor lamp, ready for the light
in the middle of the night.

The whistle on a lovely long chain,
strands of sleeplessness, knotted
with brass beads that shone
under the night light.
And he read or curled up in a heap
not to bother the partner in his bed.

The whistle was enameled
with pink chrysanthemums opened
wide against fresh green leaves,
always lined with gold edges,
always against a cold cobalt sky
even in the middle of the night.

And when you blew on
the gold-rimmed lip
the small bird, poised and ready,
always answered your call.
At night the whistle
was largely ornamental.
Someone was always there.

That day when she left for work
he raised up to say good bye;
just as the old man in the illustration
he had drawn many times before.
And she came back again
to say goodbye one more time

That day when he blew the whistle
the small bird
left the flowers
and the two were gone.

Hells with Doorbells

Should there be particular Hells
Each with a door bell to ring?
Only curiosity would tempt my ringing.
And let me stand without.
Unable to see why
Such tantalizing things
could go so wrong.

Perhaps unsuspected delays
in answering the bell
are just a well-known
sales technique to elicit temptation
Luckily, I had to catch
that last bus home.

A Chased Rose

I chased a rose
down some forgotten hill.
It knew I collected and so refused
to take a breath. It would not be used
and kept "fresh" in some poem
or even stand still.

Not be dried and saved?
Memories retained? An act
that prizes you forever---
Any dream you choose
will keep you lovely.
What's there to lose?
But it threw thorns to restore the chill

of the events following the hill, events
no rose should smooth over.
The sticking points were sharp,
lead-silver bright
that took their rightful place --meant
to save roses for days of lovers.

Days too few? Perhaps,
but the rose's priorities were right.

Wunderkammer Warehouse

On the escalator of life . . .
(no, wait-- it gets better)
one goes from floor to floor, turning
from side to side to look down on
the things that could be poems.
Clerks wave, displays beckon
but the store of not-yet-wonders
closes at ten.

If the poet dis-embarks for any
one thought there are a thousand items
to pass by at that spot,
good lines to be abandoned.

The burden of deciding,
the burden of caring enough
to make it work is not to be determined
by the size of the shopping bag.
But the wunderment of the one
singled out. And suddenly the
warehouse disappears. Nilpotent
raised to the power of me.

The sweeping view of little use
to the singularity of one small cabinet
and its items secured in poems

Heuristics of A Poet's Inspiration

First
Seek the Muse and discover she doubts
the sources of incense,
the delay of winds, the sacrificial acts.

Next stage
The Poet's Voice demands jurisdiction
and would not answer knowing others might.

Last stage
Free Choice whistled every tune
known to man
between grim laughs
for those who would be poets.

There's nothing left
but to write.

About the Author

I have found writing poetry a most
stimulating endeavor for over ten years
following my retirement from teaching in
New Mexico public schools. I have a
Doctorate in Education from Northern
Illinois University which was designed to
produce educational materials for the public
schools including film and text materials with
and for the students

 Since my retirement I have written, designed
and illustrated five chapbooks. I have have
poetry published on web zines, notably in
Snakeskin, a poetry journal edited by George
Simmers. This has been a lively exchange for
ten years with guest editing.

I hope there will be some interest in
 re-considering life's problems in the context
of some of our best literary achievements
if that doesn't sound too presumptuous.

Printed in the United States
By Bookmasters